To

Maire ...

Solidarity Books
43A Douglas Street
Cork City

Forty Four

Dana Podracká

translated from the Slovak by

Robert Welch

assisted by

Ján Gavura

Thank You For Your Visit
Paschal

SOUTHWORD*editions*

First published in 2005
by Southword Editions,
The Munster Literature Centre,
Frank O'Connor House, 84 Douglas Street,
Cork, Ireland.

Set in Garamond
Printed in Ireland by Colour Books, Dublin.

ISBN: 1-905002-10-6
www.munsterlit.ie

This book is the eighth in a series of thirteen published
as part of the official programme for Cork 2005:
European Capital of Culture
Cover Image: *Beneath the Hull* by Michael O'Donovan
42 x 53 mono screen print

Cork 2005
European Capital of Culture
RTÉ PREMIER PARTNER

Grant Aided by
Cork City Council
Comhairle Cathrach Chorcaí

the arts council
an chomhairle ealaíon

Cork County Council
1899

Contents

Beauty will Save the World
(for Fyodor Dostoyevsky)

I swore it, Fyodor Michażloviez,
as I put fresh eggs and apples
on your grave, my first time in Russia,
I swore it: beauty will save the world.

I kept dancing all night long
in a ballroom filling more and more
with love as it grew emptier,
and you were asking who I was and whom
I had met, what I had seen. And I,
just saying, beauty, beauty:
a small bird on a white stone,
its red beak, sweet bread, smiles,
the depth of Lake Baikal
in the steppes of Siberia, kissing
and sighing in Russian, saying
beauty will save the world. Mad
with emotion I embraced
the Russian (maybe Rogozhin)
snaking my limbs from head to heel all around
his body while drinking champagne,
when I touched, on his calf, like a snag
on a silver birch, the duty gun.

Beauty will save the world.

One more short throw on the roulette,
Maestro.

Beauty will save
the poor eaters of potatoes,
breathed upon by the steam of hot food,
rising like a photographic image forming
in the darkroom of lack;
will save those who eat thc sacred food
of love breathing from the steam that rises
from a warm wood after rain through which
an airship sails;
will save those who eat the last fragments
of beauty breathed out in the steam hissing
from the showerheads in the concrete gas
chambers. O Christ, I am not complaining.

Seven minutes later, the doors were opened.
Men in gas masks, men who were themselves
prisoners too, came in and carried out
the corpses, which they had to prise apart.
They had, at the last, cleaved together
in little clusters now hard to separate.

In the middle of this chalice of arms and legs
the saviour suffered,
throwing himself into the air,
to the beauty.

A Roman Elegy

There are these feelings that do not
want to go away: an alcove with seven
windows of rain; a saloon
of stuccoed walls with reliefs
of faces over
garlands of roses.
They call silence back
to the real.

And of course, too, the mug
with the image of a wolf.
Alone, in this hollow room, trying to rest
amidst hillocks of clothes piled high
on a bed supported by four indefatigable legs
with their clawed feet
I was the only prey.

I was his she-wolf, sprawled out,
taking ease after interminable toil
on a bank of the Tiber
down which his basket had sailed.

We were hooped together as in a ring.
In the despair of the one who still
is in love I call to you for help.
I think I can do this because you did not

defame me; you brought me food,
you gave me a coat of arms, a sword,
and a bench in a white church.

And you left also, in me, a resolve,
should it happen that I am expelled
from the pack, to be wolf, lone wolf.

What I Learned from Bodhan

That, when we fall in love it should be
beautiful, so that when love ends
something remains that is
mysterious.

That, although psychology can unlock
secrets of belief and unbelief,
without love nothing steady can be made
that goes on through the night.

That, in the labyrinth water will stagnate
and poison us with the minotaur of sorrow,
but that, also, only the places where it is possible
to get lost are worth the journey.

That, Uz, the land of Job, was, in the twentieth century,
the concentration camps, where God's will was amazed
by hope for a new Revelation.

That, after the Last Supper Adam and Eve got married.

That, as we believe less and less in the Heavenly
Kingdom,
we more quickly touch the lives of others,
and let them enter into us
while on this earth.

That, a poet being an animal of mythology,
it should be hunted as it runs, so
the two strongest virtues may not vanish from the
earth:
resignation and revolt.

The Re-education of Echo

You were always repeating what was said
in German or Russian or Hungarian,
hiding yourself in the language
of the strong because that of the weak
was like dried tinder, dust
igniting clay by night
with phosphorescent fear of itself:
stigmata breaking through a life.

But now, Echo, I am hunkering down with you
in a cloakroom under a rack
of empty hangers, like the arms of the many
who were hanged, before I lead you to the exit.

I have found a way of hanging on:
write like the executioner
looking for a ray of light on the face
of the victim;
write like a tomb.
You have been chosen to speak in your own voice,
clearly, with a wounded angel on your shoulder,
and above your head a light black travel bag.

Lover

A flash of light, a spike, the look
on his face reflected in the glass
as we examine the map of Katyn wood.
My desire took shape in this beginning,
a lover from that wood of mass execution.

I should not mention this,
but when we make love,
he cries out into my mouth
as he zig-zags between the trees,
running away from the shots that are aimed at him,

fleeing to her who drinks his tears
as they fall. She cries out too
as she washes the mud from her
wingéd sandals, and ascends,

light as a scream joined
in unison from the body's church.

The Catch XXII Inn

A portfire of remembrance
sparks along a wall to crimson
the colour of the inner plates
of a stove at Dachau, where you,
a porter of the dead, spent two
interminable months of despair.

And for the hundredth time you tell me
how you came through the nightmare
and began to live, how from out
of the tangled wreckage of a red Skoda
on a motorway you pulled the mangled body
of a young boy and rang for an ambulance
because to save even one was something,
dragging one out by the heels from an oven-kiln,
then holding him in your arms like the body of Christ,
waiting for the blare of the sirens.

Do not cry. Do not cry. Left lying on the roadway
a stripped coat, in a pocket a small loaf
of dandelion bread, and a copy
of the final chapter of the Book of Revelation
by St. John the Divine, Chapter XXII,
Catch XXII.

You saved him and he lives, so you may die
a happy man unless this chance is taken back.

Still Life with Predator

They released, at the plague memorial,
during the May celebrations,
doves from suitcases
with wire mesh.

We were standing by,
not living out our lives,
on our own private versions
of the travels of Ulysses;
but then there gathered
a cyclone of anguish
and a predator's eagle gaze
drove down from the sky.

It was just a shadow
that was being ripped
to shreds, just a shadow
that cried

for the things that have
happened, for what recurs,
and for what will happen again.

Some Trip

A wall, with narrow doorways sunk
into its thickness, and, when you go through,
those huge stairs ascending, a temple,
an auditorium. But this is not Macchu Picchu.
Cities without people and without graves
look like pure terror.

Look like a genius before his time;
look like a protractor, a compass,
and a hermetic book arranged upon
a stone altar of the sacrifice
in the rough energy of night.

Any moment now and Pythagoras will come
and in this dark will give a lecture
on the human implication of numbers.

Do not eat the heart.
Never step over a pair of scales.
Never rake a fire with a dagger.
Never burden or disburden.

The sum of all the numbers is 10, which is
a perfect number, and perfection is what
Earth is not, so that 10 is the final sphere
beyond the Earth and what we are.

Where we are now, this Earth,
is our love spread out and open
in the dark, and when the dawn comes
she will disappear so that the jungle
can grow back to cover all.

The Twin with the Lion Face

The trams stopped working
and people were walking in the streets,
coming down two avenues which converged,
all constantly moving, to create
a living crutch of shifting humanity.

I could not stop the conception forming
that somewhere amongst this continuous drift
I have a twin with a lion face,
a twin whom I fear as I fear a crowd,
a twin I am in hiding from,
and for whom I write.

A twin not refigured in any of the stories,
because the moment of nakedness
can never be repeated in the body's shifts,
just as fate cannot be revoked.

Fate is shaped by the hands,
just, until the skin on the tips
of the fingers wears through
to the bone.

A Shelter for Two Voices

Against the hour of your coming
I tied a rattle round my neck.

No-one knows how a tiny stone
inside a bone can calm a crying man.

Can you hear in this utter dark
the rotation of total harmony?

Do you recognize in this
a shelter for two voices?

Come inside and be safe where
I make a fire of our gentle war.

Into which I put twigs of kisses,
word-ligaments, soul-music of the bones.

In this pool of light we
become more and more abstract, Athene

leaping from the head of Zeus
into heaven, bodiless.

The Nun on the Way to Golgotha

That morning she was carrying
a plastic bag filled with bars
of soap for the monastery,
washing soap for the laundry,
little bricks towards a temple
of womanhood that will wash
smaller and change
into the purest shrouds
of Turin.

Between prayers she
ran into the shop,
fell to her knees
to pick up the soap
covered in dust, while she,
a Poor Clare, was lost
in the light of Assisi.

She left for me
a sticking plaster
that must have fallen from her
on the way, fallen for love
of the woman Gol
for the man Gotha.

The Hitchcock Hotel

A narrow carpet runner with black stripes
and bloodstains, doors without handles
standing open, plastic flowers, a shared
bathroom and toilet, the smell of fear.

Having been brought up in this anguish
I know how to bear it, lightly:
woman 1 enters, then woman 2:
daughters, mistresses, secretaries maybe.

You know the fairy tale I loved?
The one in which The Voice says: Kill Him!
She: No!
The Voice: Then kill yourself!
She: How?

Set him free.

The Silver Heron's Ascent

I read, sitting back on my heels
until my legs get stiff and I'm astonished
as the silver heron
of childhood readies for take-off.
This shy creature of the mud-flats
leaping into flight shadows
my furled expectation
as I await what flight may come
leaving behind a tiny lit-up
window

My silver heron
you make your nest in me,
please teach me to be brave
in this thick foliage of killing
and dismay. Let me be the one who's
given up to sacrifice rather than you
and you becoming lost in the four-square
silence of the place of slaughter
where no-one ever saw a wild bird cry.

She is in Love and Sleeps Among the Ruins

I am dying of love like a victim
dying of the plague. I long
so much for health that light
has painted my skin with unearthly shapes.

I am separate from everything that might
remind me of a well for water,
a dark tree containing a nest,
the fancy drinks of forbidden lust;
and I am visible
only when I am identified.

Things I haven't known till now:
that from ruins the souls, once separate,
arise, conjoin, each becoming consecrate
in the other; and jointly too they both ascend
from a river visible through the broken wall
to a sacred hill-top, where they greet the priest
who comes at last. He has been delayed
by someone needing benediction on the road
to eternity, a road so completely dire
that everything along it leads to death.

A Diary

…this hand is colder because of its distance from you.

You: I do not know if he survived

Me: Someone lifted the tablecloth covering a dead woman's body, but the corpse wasn't there. Instead there was a puppet made of bread. No-one there stood up, no-one touched the crust, as if they all knew that in every one of us someone or something has died, at least once.

You: Any true story of man and a woman cannot avoid including death. That is a rule.

Me: Have you ever killed anyone? What did you feel?

You: Nothing. It was like I was in a dream. I was young, I had a weapon. I survived, but years later….

Peter: I was in Istria. I was taking photographs. It wasn't in some bombed-out cemetery. I was in a field full of rotting pumpkins.

You: Years later. I dragged a boy from the wreckage of a crashed car, about twelve years of age. One of his eyes is reduced to a pulp. I take him in my arms and for the first time, I feel death. The dream is returning. I want to save him so badly. The ambulance is coming, it's here, but then it goes away and the motorway is empty: no cars, no people, just me alone. To this day I do not know if the boy's alive.

Peter: When Christ walked to Golgotha the thing he was carrying wasn't yet a cross. Just two pieces of wood tied with a rope. It only became a cross when they nailed him to it.

Mila: A daughter, someone's daughter is lying on a sheet, face down, so young, hair beautiful like a fall of water, silent….

Dream: Someone died. Maybe it was you. We dragged around the town at midnight, drinking from a bottle that we shared. Then someone tore off all her clothes, when the dawn came, and started running and shouting through the streets.

Mila: She lies there, not speaking. At night when I am writing trying to choose quiet words I am afraid that even they will hurt her.

Me: My daughter, although she now grown up, wants to be fed from my breasts. This hand is colder.

Mila: We must find out if he is alive.

Me: Does the intensity we create perish with us? Are we to become pure energy? Energy doesn't have consciousness, or does it?

Mila: You must find out if he's alive. But what if it is all a dream?

You: I want to live, standing on that empty motorway.

Me: There is, I know, an eternity in love. But who amongst us is capable of love? This hand is warmer because of its closeness to you.

Polishing the Glasses

I am polishing the glasses for the wine.
He will come, from the world he has created,
to the world I have formed in me.

I am wild with happiness
that we will talk
in the language of icons.

I would break my legs to get to him, allow
the palms of my hands to become soaked
with the blood of the gifts that pulse in me.

I would destroy myself, running in fiery
circles towards him at the edge of the city,
a rebel in flight from the cave of philosophers.

I am two blank eyes in a death's head
where coins can be placed to see the way
of the pilgrim, and, shining, the food it needs.

Ophelia's Bones

Yorick's grave is evergreen
and accommodating, the grave
of a Fool, testing our foolishness
with the quip of his bony question
stripped bare of tissue and skin
to the long plateau of a skull:
everything deserves to die.

    And you, Ophelia,
you are now finding it in you
to enter the big delta of oblivion,
feet-first, dreaming
against the flow.

    And how can I rebuke
you, my sister, as I kneel on the shafts
of my tibia with their little whistle-bones,
and Yorick's skull inside my head?

Eros and Homer

White on white
emerges on the black amphora
filled with the wine of life.
As if
in a kind of Braille
details come slowly into relief:
sailing ships in the night,
the shoreless face,
and then, in the middle,
the glimmering island
of an eye.

The odyssey of love is a pilgrimage
of the blind because only they
can feel out the earth and sea and sky,
come through the darkness into dark,
see what isn't there,
acquire supernatural power;

respect the wishes of the dead
and receive their sunlike blood,
go beyond the bright indigo of the actual
to find their way back.
Because Odysseus must return to Ithaca.

Danube

The damp exhalations of the river
ascend to the highest chambers
of the water tower. The pulse
of the source unfolds the heart
and lungs and there is no breaking faith
with what started in the womb,
how it was taken into the current,
revealing in the locks and cutts
tongues of evil and of good.

The river washes silt from an old
stone image I carry with me:
the priest Janko Duda stops the autobus,
gets off, goes to the tragedy on the roadway,
takes from his suitcase the confessional stole,
and with the sacred chrism of Extreme Unction
begins to administer the last rites,
kneeling down in front of the man
taken from the car that has turned over.

Amidst the shards of glass and the cherries,
in the darkening garden of blood,
he is calling with his words the spirit
of the river, and asking it to prepare
the waters of purification as well as a ship to sail
all the way down to the mouth of the delta.

Diptych with Snake

1.

My snake will die with me,
bitten with doubt;
he'll change into ashes,
death's serum.

From the very start he
was coiled around me,
sloughing off my thoughts;
he was a collar of gold,
a noose, a sword, a stick,
or a tube containing a map
of the otherworld; and he was
as absorbing as a cathedral,
a tunnel underground,
or a tomb.

Without him,
Perseus would cut off my head.

2.

And now this snake, which comes
from you, is a secret limb
of my body, knowing what I was,

so that when they wrote down all
my trials and quests and flights,
he told me I was his loved one,
his desire, and planted for me
vineyards, made plentiful with fish
the streams, and threw richness
to the stars.

He took me to those
places where woman cannot go, the chamber
of male ecstasy where Medusa stares
and wants to offer him her head.

Fetch

You will look and I won't be there
anymore, no more perhaps than
a fragment of ancient verse.

But this happened to me, many times–
in the underpass covered in graffiti
that recalled testament, declaration;
or on a ferry, helping to carry
glass shelters to the opposite bank:
I was the fetch of a sister who had
long ago left the country, a girl ruined
by love, or a *femme fatale* coming back
from some deep ravine.

Faces full of misapprehension
and mistake tried to hold on to me,
attached like bark to a tree
that wasn't there. Meanwhile I,
on board ship but separate from the crew,
was ready to jump overboard, to save the story
that wanted to survive, and was looking for
the mouth of Jonah's whale.

This is the tale where every shipwreck,
cast up on a lonely shore,
waits for the resurrection,
and the flying fish of the word.

A Hair from your Mother's Head

A window shutter smashes open and shut
in the night while the beast
of sleeplessness furls and unfurls
the wings of the moon.

There is a hoar-frost in the room
and an angel sits at the edge of the bed.
You are sleeping and dreaming of a man
in a hat of crystal: Kristallnacht.

The flats upstairs are empty
but the chandeliers are trembling.
You are in David's abyss and you shout
as you reach up with two hands to catch

a hair of your mother's head. Then you're
set down on a station platform where
the freight wagons vanish into the dawn
that is the fading lamp of my body,

my love.

A Man from the Underground

He has, this man from the underground,
the elongation of wings
in a ladder of wrinkles
that lead up to a world of light above his eyes.

Marked and starred by the honorifics
of the sun he and his confréres
set to rights the sad worlds
of the betrayed, the enslaved,
those who are killed,
entries in mislaid or casual records:
like traces of moonblood never before found
in desk-drawers or in the torn leather of armchairs.

As difficult to trace as
Nietzsche's spirit in the Alps,
or the music of Sappho's lyre
on Lesbos where the wild goats roam.

This man plots the movement of a thought
finding for it a way through the crowd
that divides; he is like someone who walks
on long stilts, a ghost,
balancing beauty, cajolery, and fear,

calling them out of the thin air
from way above his head,
and from way deep down below.

A Parcel from Prison

I, a political prisoner, confirm
by the signature below, that I have consigned
to the state all my personal and civic possessions
and that I have no formal requests to make
to the authorities. I also declare that,
while under escort I lost one handkerchief,
possibly at the time of my arrest.
I agree to the following items being struck from the list:

a pair of broken spectacles in a case
an old hand brush
a neckerchief
a pair of mittens
a chessboard with pieces
another 4 handkerchiefs
12 books
application forms for a retrial
a Ziak fountain pen

Leave to me just enough strength
to fight free of the snares of misgiving
when the sun falls before sunset
on the grey concrete floor summoning
the shadows that wait to greet me.

A White Bedsheet

I could only write it with the white
graphite pencil of the blind, white
on a white sheet that is a blank
mouth to swallow every word so that
I can recall only the essential part,
the skull of it:

Belbo: I hope you do not think that when
Rabbis speak about the Torah
they mean just the scroll,
the words inscribed thereon.
The Torah is really us, those who
use the language so as to change
the nature of the body. Change
what is written in the Book
and you modify the world and when
you modify the world you will change
the nature of your body.

Belbo, please, don't leave. Say
if change is only possible alone,
or can it be accomplished with someone
else, a partner, the two roped
together like a pair of mountaineers?

Like Rembrandt to his paintings,
or Nietzsche to his Christ.

Or like the starving little girls,
Anna and Maria, who with two hands clasped
each other, and with the other two prayed
that their bodies might be changed to bread
to improve the world; which they would wrap
in a white sheet in a double cross
which needs to be bleached in the sun.

Letting Go

I am lying in the bed of seven senses,
and I am letting go, into the waves of cold
that drive up from the soles of my feet
to the hinterland behind the bedstead,

your body out of mine:
the meadows of fingers, mineral deposits
of hands, wooded hills and valleys,
and underneath the cavernous structures

of bone-roots. But you are kneeling above me,
begging me not to do this; again and again
coming down to the caverns,
seeking the well-heads.

Just as when I last gave you the harvest
of love, the ripe terror of our domain,
which was: you can do whatever you want,
your soul is mine.

Deepsong

I'm a skeleton (female)
and when I sleep with a man
I possess his body,
then his heart with its
blood sap; I sigh
in his mouth in a thought–
beat, then talk in one
of the Biblical languages.
After which succumbing
there is deepsong.

Guided by a little white
map of the Styx I move
in you from forehead
to belly and know what
you are: a yearning to
be the sacral bone from which
the spine is to rise.
You plough the black soil
of becoming, that is nothing,
in which under our fingers
grow living and actual flowers.

A Woman and her Soul

She is always falling, since she was a child,
and barefoot without shinguards she's flown
over those dreams: the alphabet of grass-snakes,
the well with a lit skull, an office containing a

blue wing. Following none it was she
who was followed: while reading Robert Graves,
trying to figure what Goya meant about Madrid,
or while offering lonely encouragement
to Martinovicz's men when they were put to death
at the Bloody Field.

When she spoke her face was visible,
like a round moon thrown to wolves.

She was receiving messages out of quartz
and from the wind that smote her back
up on the high plains in order that she night find
a language she could share with the horizon.

She suffered a number of defeats – a checkmate,
a Waterloo, but she was granted asylum,
and a choke-chain.

She sought a hexahedron of solitude where
she could recognize her negatives for what they were,

and not forego what had been given to her,
including limewash for a fresco.

Exile could be regarded as an eviction to the isle
of the blessed, where she could be happy,
know bliss plated by having been dipped
into the silver of sadness, and be immersed
in the glow of lights in the distance.

When she disentangled herself from that net
for two she'd become involved in, she was not
easy on herself as she fought free of intricacies
of longing and doublecross. This so she could come
to see what her dowry had been.

From this inventory and naming it must be clear
this one does not belong completely
to anyone or any place.

The Creation of Your Own Language

Potholes and the unabashed and unpruned
tops of trees accompanied us on
the illicit and secret night journey
we took to Vladimir to see 'The Day
of Judgement' by the great Andrei Rublyov.
(We should have paid in dollars, but didn't.)

Refugees from the official language,
we seek asylum in the language of
the interior. It is cold, remote, and holy,
like a golden spoon in a display case,
never used for eating.

Break the glass, remove the merchants that are
in you, but anyway, pay the highest price.

Giving Thanks
(after Jean-Baptiste Millet)

From the morning to the evening bell
and at the Angelus I am filled
with a wave of gratitude and my whole
body gives thanks again and again.

And for no reason, for no one.
It happens in the middle of a dug up street,
looking at a display of books in a window,
when snow and rain fall together and leaves

stick to my shoes. I stop short and give
thanks, finding myself in Millet's painting
with a tree as my partner in devotion,
a navvy, the man behind the bookshop counter,

a shovel, and a piece of timber board. Note
this: the Twin Towers in New York, what
were they but skyscraper versions
of two companions in a picture by Millet?

I give thanks until the freeze is over,
and at night when I lie down and switch off
the lamp, deep down in the distance
a light goes on in my womb.

The Love of Barbara Stein

That other one in me, the hidden,
the one that cries out for help,
checked into the Hotel Pro Patria
under the name of Barbara Stein,

She is ten years older than me,
and she knows the seat of the Hapsburgs;
she drove the first ever motor car
and survived a death camp.

She learned how to love without prejudice
because she had to die a number of times,
being contaminated by the gold
sheen beneath her skin.

You cannot ever get to know her
because she doesn't want the pity
of your love; she wants the way you think
to be entirely yours, like

fox meat, which, when they have flayed
the beast, no-one will eat for fear
of rabies, of passion, which would cause,
unbearably, the wall to subside.

The Squared Notebooks

On the squared grille of the confessional
my soul has inscribed its record.
Years have been spent divulging an inner
time and I have put it away in a small
case where valuables are kept.

As a confession it leaves a lot to be
desired: no initials, no periods;
sometimes I am adamant, sometimes
totally insecure:

    a bodybag containing Dubček at Ruzyne
                                        airport;
    a supreme encounter that leaves me reeling like
                                        I'm seasick;
    the Gospels are bodiless;
    if I allow love I allow deceit.

This record speaks of what has happened,
and also of what will happen.
Everything is hidden behind words,
because they are the sweet morsels
of the first forbidden fruit, which,
as soon as man put it into his mouth
he started to long for meat.

The Creaking Gate of your Heart

The warm breath of your palms
has opened an ear in me so
for the first time I can hear
your heartbeat, the loosely locked
gate of your heart with its soft creak,
a delaying echo behind the song,
an octave above. Through this gate
I can smoothly enter your house.

In a chamber to the left Piero Della Francesca's
painting at Montcherchi of the pregnant
Madonna, the girl in a blue robe,
in the chapel for the dead. On the fresco, too,
depicted in the folds, the oldest map
of the river Styx, showing the way
to death through a mother's womb.

Between the thousandth and thousandth-
and-first kiss, the most complete
realization of the spaces in a woman's
body, I flow through you, breathlessly,
loving you to the uttermost;
and I ask the one who is inside you
to not let your hour come before mine.

So that we can in mutuality
arrange a complete exchange of texts.

So death can rewrite them as fair copies
with ink made of leaves, with a hand of flame.

Still Life with a Rabbi's Cap

I have, dear Rabbi, in me too much
of the sun, a measure running over
which forces me to welcome fear
along with beauty:
a crumb of matzo bread, flour and water,
a symmetrical place of remembrance
with non-existent graves.

So much. So much.
I can confide in you, dear Rabbi,
because you know so well how precious
is that which goes beyond measure to excess:
words, seeds, blood,
so much blood.

And because there was also so much fear,
it too became holy.

Like the three nails in the hands and feet,
like the stars on a dress rising in the sky
when the body has gone.

A Glass of Water

I was awakened in the black of night
by a voice, in my sleep, pleading
for a glass of water.

Even now I can still hear it, the quiet
persistence of that cry
coming from the membrane of the soft
fontanelle in a child's open skull,
from a sick bed,
or from the cracked ground beneath
a pilgrim's feet.

I got up, went through to the kitchen,
filled a glass of water, and drank,
for the thirsty one who,

no longer in the body,
was finding it very hard
to do anything without assistance.

Teaching to Vision

There it was, in a gauche and callow
piece of cinema, a plastic bag air–
lifting from the cobblestones, swell-
ing from the windgust, giving itself up
to flight, dancing its flamenco
before a kiosk in front of the windows
of the Mother Teresa Hospital.

For all the world a soul,
the radiant swirl of a nebula
in which was joined:

the blueprint for a temple,
the interrogation of a political prisoner,
a bowl fallen out of someone's hands rolling across the floor.

I am weak, my soul, when I see
how you run across the white stones
to someone's heart, always
to the heart.

A Wafer of Love

I keep your name in a little jar behind my bed
ever since you passed it from your mouth
to mine to enter the river of my body
so that you will surface on the strand of my heart
to live out there an island life.

You write from Jericho describing for me
a ruined apartment there where stands
a bed of cherrywood, as in the *Odyssey*:
by the living trunk of the bedpost you say
we eat a white gingerbread
containing a tiny mirror
and have one face.

And this is enough for me to find the courage
to hold my breath and swim to you inside myself,
underwater; before I reach your level
you will see, beneath the surface,
the moon of a face,
a wafer of loving communion.

Colonel of the Death Cavalry

(for Zbigniew Herbert)

You are writing it down: you say
poetry is a breviary where the poet,
with no mask, looks each of us in the eye.
He could not speak, he gibbered
as his voice struggled to reach his mouth
but it flowed out through a hole in his neck.
He wasn't Mr Cogito or any of his others
any more and an identification tag bore
the name which he had written: 'Herbert,
Colonel of the Death Cavalry.'

I am sorry, dear mentor, but I don't agree.
The encounter with a genius always involves
a bizarre redemption of the self;
and you, you as well, though you will
falter and forget, yet you will dream
about the long road to Venice
where love holds sway over black death.

And where hope still happens,
that there may be the encounter with love
as she hails with her black-gloved hand a gondola,
filling with quickening light.

The Guardian of the Spring

In the silence of Štiavnica's hills
a guardian spirit keeps watch beneath
a clear well of spring water,
deep below its open mouth.

The space around is a circle
of glowering energy where you might see
golden gates emblazoned with the legend:
'chip chop cherry, come inside and you'll be sorry'.

It was here that someone came to brazen out
his loutishness, broke the glass
on a washed-out picture of the Virgin
nailed to the trunk of a spruce.

Someone who, for his own reasons, needed to take
the enameled mug on the rock.

Someone else, it seems, came after,
to clean mushrooms and throw worms in the water.

Guardian of the well, you who are sprung
from the sacred womb of the galaxy,
who surges in all the sources of water
and of energy, you soar
beneath the well-spring of the sky.

Please, we ask you, stay vigilant,
as love does, when it lies down on a bed of needles
and cries.

The Last Rest of Adam and Eve

We have the dry leaves to cover us,
a fire of burnt bark under the bent pines,
once struck by lightening,
that incline to the white bedrock
on this northern side
where a shadow is playing with a squirrel,
and a snake dies when the sun goes down.

Tomorrow I will betray you. At dawn
I will try the winter fruit of your womb,
step into the presence and expulsion
of knowledge. Which will herd us into pastures
of bitter grass, stop us on the road,
and eat into our senses.

Forgive me, my love.

I am asking you, do not let me do anything.

Journey of the Famished Soul

Different now, I am like those who pass through
the dark wood, dip a finger of quiet
into a cleft of the rock,
drink deep
of the water and wine
from the given chalice
of unease.

Things start to go strange
for those who drink:
they get the feel of the clay they are of,
in a gold shaft of wafer-thin light;
they catch fish to feed,
before setting out on the long road,
the famished soul.

Which will come, at last, to the point,
the destination, where in the secret cage
a lordly ear inclines to the words
once written from the vantage of love
out of the stream's eddy,
in the sign.

Antigone and the Wretches

Chrous Leader: It is our sacred duty to give
due honour to death;
and it is not possible
to resist the power
of authority.

Antigone: I have set one hope and that is
that once there in death
I will be good to my father
and my mother, and kind to you
my dear brother!
It was I who, when you died,
washed and dressed you
with my own hands,
and made the offerings for you
on your grave.
I, a virgin,
who has never heard her wedding-chant,
must leave this life alive.

Who is reading here? Who pays heed
to those poor wretches who, when night falls,
look for a conduit carrying warm water,
a stretch of that concrete paradise of heat
connecting two metres below ground level?

If it is you Antigone who reads, come.
We have saved for you a length
of clean bandage so you can clean
your tin begging-bowl. Look!
Can you see in its sheen
an assembly of the hungry and unwashed,
all asleep together in the camp
clutching their spoons under a vacant sky.

Each one of them, every one,
will have to be buried in the river
freezing now to two feet deep.
Their knees will bulge from the ice
like fir-cones.
Each one of them will have had placed
under the tongue the marzipan sweetmeat
of beginning before heading to
the fearsome tunnel's entrance.

Duras Among the Seabirds

I wanted to have a drink with you,
Marguerite, when I recognised you
among the seabirds drifting over
libraries of sand.
Words leave imprints on people,
limping texts, fiction.

At the bar in the harbour
you cried out your song:
that writing is a power to destroy,
can get beneath the skin,
may remove the eyes and the mouth,
and then require a face.

Writing is Dachau's command square
on white paper.
Without it, it being love,
all questions are senseless.

The Place of Execution of the First President

Thank you, Lord, for the gift of sadness
that brought me even past the metal door
into the cell where they hanged our president
and where now they kennel dogs in cages.

I can hear them barking and then their howling
fades to a quiet that succeeds in which
a silver chalice is lifted up, the final Mass
is being said behind the metal door,
and there is a last breaking and sharing of bread.

Thank you, Lord, for the gift of shame
in which the dog-handler told us of the lime-pit,
a place in the yard where you could see
the sunrise, as he tried to hide, in the pocket
of his uniform, his ten o'clock snack.